Catchwords Orange

Charles Cripps

Third E

illustrated by Allan Stomann,
Katrina van Gendt
and Philip Eldridge

HBJ Harcourt Brace Jovanovich, Publishers
London   Sydney   Orlando   Toronto

UK edition published by
Harcourt Brace Jovanovich Limited
24/28 Oval Road, London NW1 7DX

Copyright © 1990, 1988, 1983, 1978 by
Harcourt Brace Jovanovich
Group (Australia) Pty Limited

Printed in the United Kingdom

ISBN 0 7466 0025 9

LOOK

COVER

WRITE

CHECK

When learning to spell these words you must always:

LOOK

Look carefully at the word so that you remember what you have seen.

COVER

Cover the word with a piece of card.

WRITE

Write the word from memory.

CHECK

Check that you have written the word correctly.

If you have not written the word correctly start again. Look at the word. Cover it and write it from memory. Then check your spelling.

1 The following words are important as you use them in your
TABLES OF MEASURES for MASS, LENGTH, AREA and VOLUME.

milligram   millimetre   millilitre

                     centimetre

gram   metre   litre

kilogram   kilometre   kilolitre

You will also need the following additional words.

square   cubic

tonne   hectare

These ideas may help you to remember these words.

1. Look carefully at these words and write them from memory.

gram . . . .

metre . . . .

litre . . . .

2. Look carefully at these beginnings and write them from
    memory.

micro . . . .

milli . . . .

kilo . . . .

mega . . . .

3. You will also need to practise these additional words.

square . . . .

cubic . . . .

tonne . . . .

hectare . . . .

2

one	first
two	second
three	third
four	fourth
five	fifth
six	sixth
seven	seventh
eight	eighth
nine	ninth
ten	tenth
eleven	eleventh
twelve	twelfth
thirteen	thirteenth
fourteen	fourteenth
fifteen	fifteenth
sixteen	sixteenth
seventeen	seventeenth
eighteen	eighteenth
nineteen	nineteenth
twenty	twentieth
thirty	
forty	
fifty	
sixty	
seventy	
eighty	
ninety	
hundred	

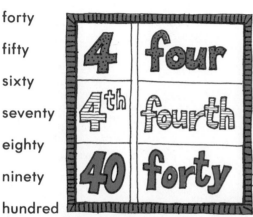

Number words like **first**, **second**, and **third** tell the order of things. Many of these words are made by adding **th** to a number word.

four + th = fourth

A letter is dropped before **th** is added to **eight** and **nine**.

eigh(t) + th = eigh( )th = eighth

nin(e) + th = nin( )th = ninth

Look at the word **fifth**. What happens to **five** to make **fifth**?

REMEMBER THIS: There is a **u** in **four**, **fourth** and **fourteen**, but not in **forty**.

3 Look carefully at the word for each DAY OF THE WEEK.

Now look at the letter pattern in bold print and at the other words containing the same letter pattern. You may already know these words. If so they will help you to remember the DAYS OF THE WEEK.

Monday ....

month ....

money ....

monkey ....

Tu**es**day ....

blues ....

glues ....

Wed**nes**day ....

nest ....

Th**urs**day ....

purse ....

nurse ....

Friday ....

friend ....

fright ....

Satur**day** . . . .

turn . . . .

turnip . . . .

sturdy . . . .

Sunday . . . .

sung . . . .

sunk . . . .

When you have looked carefully at each word, cover it and
write the word from memory.

Check your answer.

Now try these.

1. Write the full names for these abbreviations.

    Wed. _____   Tues. _____

    Sat. _____   Thurs. _____

    Mon. _____   Sun. _____

    Fri. _____

2. Write the days that come before and after Wednesday.

    _____   _____

3. Finish the poem.

    On Monday I'm quiet,

    On Tuesday I speak.

    I do something different

    Each day of the _____.

4 You may like to learn these words by looking carefully at the
smaller words in them.

Easter . . . .

Christmas . . . .

5 January February March April May June July
August September October November December

The following suggestions may help you to remember the
MONTHS OF THE YEAR. Look at the letter patterns and then
cover and write the words.

Jan
Febr } uary

....

....

Sept
Nov } ember
Dec

....

....

....

Septem
Octo
Novem } ber
Decem

....

....

....

....

Ma { rch
        y

....

....

Ju { ne
        ly

....

....

The words **apron** and **apricot**
may help you to remember **April**.

....

....

The word **Autumn**
may help you to remember **August**.

....

....

1. January
2. February
3. March
4. April
5. May
6. June
7. July
8. August
9. September
10. October
11. November
12. December
13. Jan.
14. Feb.
15. Mar.
16. Apr.
17. Aug.
18. Sept.
19. Oct.
20. Nov.
21. Dec.

SPELL-O-GRAM

CODE	WORDS	CH G	TIME	DATE	TO:
INSTRUCTIONS					

WHAT MONTH AM I?

My first letter is in **FIT,** but not in **BIT.**
My second's in **LET,** but not in **LOT.**
My third's in **BONE, but not in CONE.**
My fourth is in **ARE,** but not in **ATE.**
My fifth is in **BUT,** but not in **BAT.**
My sixth is in **WATCH,** but not in **WITCH.**
My seventh is in **CROWN,** but not in **CLOWN.**
My eighth is in **MY,** but not in **ME.**
I am the month of _ _ _ _ _ _ _ _ .

SENDER'S NAME

FOR OFFICE USE ONLY

The answer to this "Spell-o-gram" is *February*. You can write your own Spell-o-grams for the other months.

The names of the months are proper nouns. Proper nouns begin with capital letters.

February   **S**eptember

The names of the months are often written as abbreviations. An **abbreviation** is a short way of writing a word.

Feb.   Sept.

Abbreviations of the months begin with capital letters and end with full stops. Three months are not abbreviated: May, June, and July.

Write the names of the months that come before and after each month.

1. _____ November _____

2. _____ February _____

3. _____ March _____

4. _____ September _____

5. Write the four names of months that do not have the letter **r**.

_____   _____

_____   _____

6. Write the three names of months that have no abbreviations.

_____   _____   _____

Write the abbreviations for these names of months.

7. March _____   8. October _____   9. August _____

10. February _____   11. December _____   12. January _____

13. November _____   14. September _____   15. April _____

Finish the poem with the full names of months.

Thirty days has (Sept.) _16_,

(Apr.) _17_, June, and (Nov.) _18_.

All the rest have thirty-one,

Save (Feb.) _19_, which alone

Has twenty-eight. And one day more

We add to it one year in four.

16. _____

17. _____

18. _____

19. _____

WORDS IN TIME

Centuries ago, people who studied the stars named a red planet after Mars, the Roman god of war. This star appeared in the third month of the year. They called that month *Martium*, 'belonging to Mars'. *March* comes from the Roman name.

7 Look carefully at the following words.

bundle

copper

curly

goodbye

enemy

lantern

Complete each question by writing the correct word.

Write the word beginning with **cop**.   . . . .

Write the word ending with **ye**.   . . . .

Write the word with **ant** in it.   . . . .

Write the word beginning with **bun**.   . . . .

Write the word ending with **ly**.   . . . .

Write the word with **nem** in it.   . . . .

8 Look carefully at **side**. Now try to write **aside**.   _____   _____

Now do the same for the following.

oil	boil	. . . .
ill	bill	. . . .
print	sprint	. . . .
hip	whip	. . . .
rice	price	. . . .
lash	flash	. . . .
lock	flock	. . . .
king	smoking	. . . .
stem	system	. . . .
table	vegetables	. . . .

9 Practise writing the **sp** letter pattern.

Now make some new words by adding this pattern to the words in the boxes.

sp

| ace |
| are |
| ice |
| in |
| lash |
| lit |
| rain |

------------ ------------

. . . .

. . . .

. . . .

. . . .

. . . .

. . . .

. . . .

10 Practise writing the **ca** letter pattern.

Now use it to begin the following words.

ca

| se |
| ke |
| me |
| ge |
| ne |
| pe |
| fe |
| re |

------------ ------------

. . . .

. . . .

. . . .

. . . .

. . . .

. . . .

. . . .

. . . .

11 Practise writing the **wr** letter pattern.

Now use it to begin the following words.

wr

| ist |
| ong |
| ap |
| eck |
| eath |

------------ ------------

. . . .

. . . .

. . . .

. . . .

. . . .

12 Look carefully at the word in brackets at the end of each sentence.

Use this word to help you spell the word missing from each sentence.

I heard the teacher growl, _____ you can do better than that!'

(sure)

The baby _____ during most of the journey. **(cries)**

For how many hours did it rain last _____? **(eve)**

After the swim they decided to get _____ and go home for tea.

(dresses)

The boy was _____ to get his clothes wet playing in the rain.

(fool)

Was there more _____ in the school during first or last term?

(sick)

13 Look carefully at **lame**. Now try to write **flame**.   _____   _____

Now do the same for the following.

deed	indeed	. . . .
horn	thorn	. . . .
hook	shook	. . . .
heel	wheel	. . . .
like	alike	. . . .
heap	cheap	. . . .
cream	scream	. . . .
table	stable	. . . .
rain	sprain	. . . .
sing	closing	. . . .

14 Change the **c** in **coat** for **b, g, fl** and **thr**.

. . . .

. . . .

. . . .

. . . .

Change the **p** in **pole** for **h, wh** and **st**.

. . . .

. . . .

. . . .

Change the **d** in **dumb** for **cr** and **th**.

. . . .

. . . .

Change the **s** in **saying** for **p, l, pl** and **sw**.

. . . .

. . . .

. . . .

Change the **p** in **patch** for **h, scr** and **w**.

. . . .

. . . .

Change the **b** in **boss** for **l, m** and **cr**.

. . . .

. . . .

. . . .

Change the **c** in **cape** for **t, g** and **sh**.

. . . .

. . . .

15 The words in a dictionary are listed in alphabetical order. To put words in alphabetical order, use the first letter of each word. If the first letters are the same, use the second letter to put words in alphabetical order. If the second letters are the same use the third letter. If the first three letters are the same use the fourth letter.

Write each list of words in alphabetical order.

drift _____   bury _____

prevent _____   tie _____

pretend _____   burn _____

drill _____   tied _____

dries _____   burst _____

prepare _____   ties _____

ALPHABET TRAIL

a o
b p
c q
d r
e s
f t
g u
h v
i w
j x
k y
l m z
n

16 Look carefully at the word in brackets at the end of each sentence.

Use this word to help you spell the word missing from each sentence.

Somebody said they _____ into their new house last Friday. **(moving)**

They were angry because they had been _____ at the bus stop for over an hour. **(sit)**

The farmers all _____ for heavy rain to save their crops. **(pray)**

Those boats were _____ very fast across the bay. **(raced)**

Tell me who has broken my new plastic _____! **(rule)**

17   Look carefully at the word in bold print.

Now look at all the smaller words in this word.

slippery

slip

lip

slipper

Can you write all these words from memory?

Now do the same with these words.

teacher

tea

teach

each

ache

he

her

thinking

thin

in

ink

think

kin

king

every

eve

ever

very

18

coat	thanked	undo	harvest
coast	ankle	until	carve
coach	blanket	unless	starve

All these words are in the jumbled sentences below. Remember, a sentence begins with a capital letter and ends with a full stop. Now write the sentences.

1. roadaway.Thefollowedlongcoastthesuchforcoach

_____

2. thankedherbringingfriendwarmMaryblanket.thefor

_____

3. shinesnothingharvest.Unlesstothehavewilloursunfarmerspoor

_____

4. meat.cannotcarveWeuntileatyouthe

_____

5. Timbandagetheankle.hisaskedtoundonotaroundwas

_____

6. school.alwaysgirltoSundayTheacoatwore

_____

7. starvewillunlessthemfood.Incountriesmanypoorsendwepeople

_____

8. footballcoachISteveifcouldaskedteam.our

_____

19 By changing some letters in one word you can easily make new words.

Now follow the instructions carefully and see what happens.

Write the word **rough**. . . . .

Change the **r** to **c**. . . . .

Change the **c** to **b**. . . . .

Add a **t** to the end. . . . .

Change the **b** to **f**. . . . .

Change the **f** to **th**. . . . .

Write the word **good**. . . . .

Change the **g** to **h**. . . . .

Change the **h** to **f**. . . . .

Insert an **l** after the **f**. . . . .

Change the **f** to **b**. . . . .

Write the word **home**. . . . .

Change the **me** to **se**. . . . .

Change the **h** to **n**. . . . .

Change the **se** to **ne**. . . . .

Change the **o** to **i**. . . . .

Add **ty** to the end. . . . .

20 know tack king now order own kin no attack start
in interest art sting to pass sing toes hopping in
mat ass in to star inter tin record or tacking cord
in at known tar resting in tart tomato shop pin toe
at sin hop ping as rest tin in

These words are hidden in the longer words below. See if you
can put each word under the longer word in which it is hidden.
Use each word once only and cross it off as you use it.

shopping

_____

_____

_____

_____

_____

attacking

_____

_____

_____

_____

_____

_____

unknown

_____

_____

_____

_____

_____

tomatoes

_____

_____

_____

_____

_____

_____

_____

recorder

_____

_____

_____

_____

passing

_____

_____

_____

_____

starting

_____

_____

_____

_____

_____

_____

interesting

_____

_____

_____

_____

_____

21 Look carefully at the letter pattern in each box and use it to
end the following words.

b
m ⟩ utton

dr
sw ⟩ ift

g
w ⟩ olf

cr
tr ⟩ ust

cr
ch ⟩ ew

k
scr ⟩ een

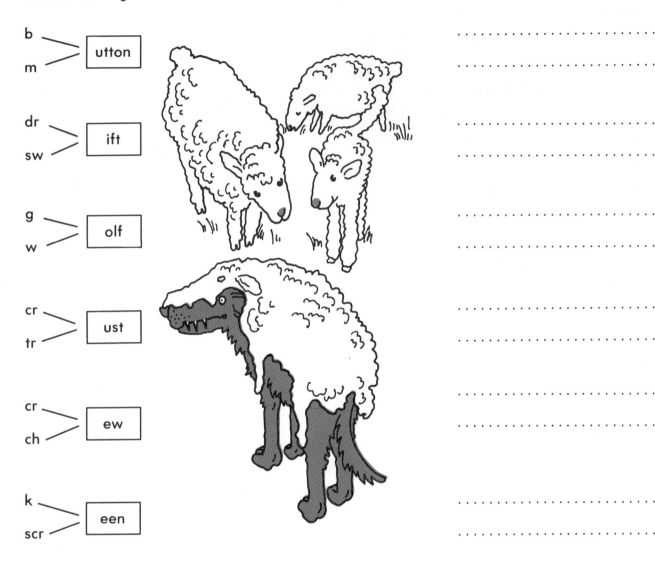

. . . .

. . . .

. . . .

. . . .

. . . .

. . . .

. . . .

. . . .

. . . .

. . . .

22 Practise writing the **ea** letter pattern.

Now use it to begin the following words.

ch
st
ea ⟨ sy
se
gle

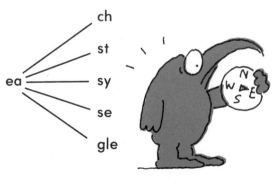

_____   _____

. . . .

. . . .

. . . .

. . . .

23 Look carefully at the following words. Each one has a smaller
word in it. This smaller word may help you to remember the
longer word.

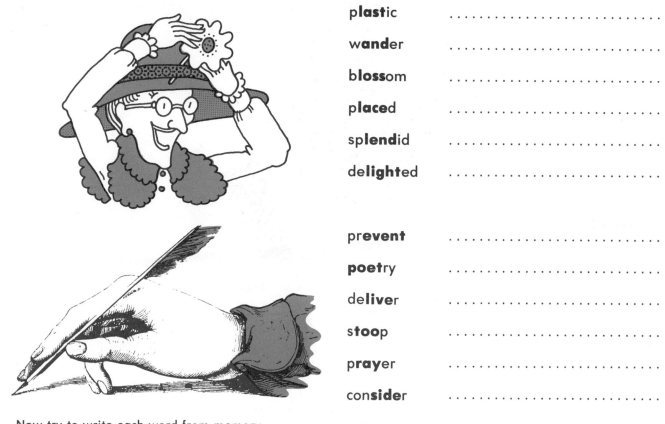

p**last**ic ....

w**and**er ....

b**loss**om ....

p**lace**d ....

sp**lend**id ....

de**ligh**ted ....

pr**event** ....

poetry ....

de**liv**er ....

s**too**p ....

p**ray**er ....

con**side**r ....

Now try to write each word from memory.

24 Look carefully at the following words. Find the word families
and write them in the boxes.

works ....

wishes ....

likes ....

wished ....

worked ....

liked ....

working ....

wishing ....

liking ....

25 Look carefully at the following words.

ago

apron

bacon

bait

kettle

fuel

Complete each question by writing the correct word.

Write the word with **g** in the middle. ....

Write the word beginning with **f**. ....

Write the word ending with **con**. ....

Write the word with **ai** in it. ....

Write the word with **pro** in it. ....

Write the word with **tt** in it. ....

26 Look carefully at the following words. Find the word families and write them in the boxes.

reads

shown

rainy

showed

rained

reader

raining

showing

reading

27 Many words have other words hidden within them. If you can find these words they may help you to remember the first word.

Look at the example below and then try to break down the other words.

climbing

climb

 limb

   bin

    in

millimetre

therefore

splashed

tramping

thanked

vegetables

seventeen

whenever

wheat

28 You can build your own word pyramids by following the directions below.

Begin with the first word and then make longer and longer words by adding one letter at a time.

Write the word **on**.

Add an **e** to the end.

Begin with a **t**.

Begin with an **s**.

Add an **s** to the end.

Write the word **oar**.

Begin with a **b**.

Add a **d** to the end.

Begin with an **a**.

29 Look carefully at the word in brackets at the end of each sentence.

Use this word to help you spell the word missing from each sentence.

During the storm dozens of small boats were _____ out to sea. **(sweep)**

Will the farmer be _____ a tractor every day next week? **(used)**

They _____ the water off when they went on holiday. **(turning)**

The _____ child in the class was chosen to play the part. **(smaller)**

My country cousin was _____ this weekend. **(comes)**

30 Look carefully at the letter pattern in each box and use it to end the following words.

fr ⟩ ☐ ied
tr ⟩

_____

_____

str ⟩ ☐ ike
al ⟩

_____

_____

t ⟩ ☐ ooth
sm ⟩

_____

_____

tom ⟩ ☐ ato
pot ⟩

_____

_____

h ⟩ ☐ aving
s ⟩

_____

_____

f ⟩ ☐ olk
y ⟩

_____

_____

sh ⟩ ☐ ining
d ⟩

_____

_____

k ⟩ ☐ ept
cr ⟩

_____

_____

d ⟩ ☐ ense
s ⟩

_____

_____

sc ⟩ ☐ ale
wh ⟩

_____

_____

b ⟩ ☐ orrow
s ⟩

_____

_____

b ⟩ ☐ olt
c ⟩

_____

_____

31 Look carefully at the following words. Find the word families and write them in the boxes.

step

fishes

fished

steps

fishing

stepped

stepping

fisherman

```
. . . . . . . . . . . . . . . . . . . . .
. . . . . . . . . . . . . . . . . . . . .
. . . . . . . . . . . . . . . . . . . . .
. . . . . . . . . . . . . . . . . . . . .
. . . . . . . . . . . . . . . . . . . . .
. . . . . . . . . . . . . . . . . . . . .
. . . . . . . . . . . . . . . . . . . . .
. . . . . . . . . . . . . . . . . . . . .
```

32 Practise writing the word **see**.

Now use it to begin the new words.

```
        k
        n
see
        d
        med
```

```
_____    _____

. . . . . . . . . . . . . . . . . . . . .
. . . . . . . . . . . . . . . . . . . . .
. . . . . . . . . . . . . . . . . . . . .
. . . . . . . . . . . . . . . . . . . . .
```

33 The words in a dictionary are listed in alphabetical order. To put words in alphabetical order, use the first letter of each word. If the first letters are the same, use the second letter to put words in alphabetical order. If the second letters are the same use the third letter.

Write each list of words in alphabetical order.

seek	_____	wolf	_____
taste	_____	king	_____
seemed	_____	wore	_____
tart	_____	kind	_____
seed	_____	wolves	_____
tar	_____	kill	_____

34 Look carefully at the following words. Find the word families
and write them in the boxes.

looked

played

loved

player

looks

lovely

playing

loving

looking

. . . .
. . . .
. . . .
. . . .
. . . .
. . . .
. . . .
. . . .

35 Look carefully at the following words.

bench

bubble

umpire

simple

traffic

verse

Complete each question by writing the correct word.

Write the word with **ff** in it.   . . . .

Write the word ending with **ch**.   . . . .

Write the word with **er** in it.   . . . .

Write the word beginning with **um**.   . . . .

Write the word with **bb** in it.   . . . .

Write the word beginning with **s**.   . . . .

36 Look carefully at the word in brackets at the end of each sentence.

Use this word to help you spell the word missing from each sentence.

Does the old brick _____ still make the best fresh bread? **(bakes)**

Kristy _____ up her work because she wanted to start again. **(torn)**

We heard the pack of _____ howling all through the night. **(wolf)**

After the practice match, most of the team hoped the coach would _____ them. **(chosen)**

_____ a snow-covered mountain can be dangerous! **(climb)**

37 Sometimes two words are put together to make a new word. This new word is called a compound word.

Join these pieces together to make compound words.

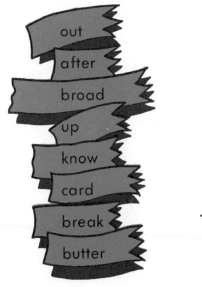 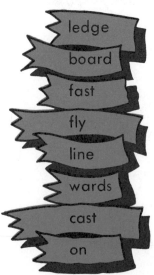

. . . .

. . . .

. . . .

. . . .

. . . .

. . . .

. . . .

. . . .

38 Practise writing the **ness** letter pattern.

Now make some new words beginning with the letters in the boxes.

| good |
| dark | → ness
| har |
| kind |

Single Goat or Dog Harness.
Red Leather, Fire Department Style.
$2.70
No. 10R830
Weight, about 3 pounds.

_____ _____

. . . .

. . . .

. . . .

. . . .

39 Practise writing the **ain** letter pattern.

Now make some new words beginning with the letters in the boxes.

| rem |
| spr | → ain
| br |
| expl |

_____ _____

. . . .

. . . .

. . . .

. . . .

40 Practise writing the **rade** letter pattern.

Now make some new words beginning with the letters in the boxes.

| g |
| t | → rade
| pa |

_____ _____

. . . .

. . . .

. . . .

41 Practise writing the **ake** letter pattern.

Now make some new words beginning with the letters in the boxes.

| c |
| aw | → ake
| mist |

_____ _____

. . . .

. . . .

. . . .

42 Use the letter pattern at the top of each box to make new words.

uck	ull	ack	ure
tr _____	b _____	cr _____	p _____
l _____	p _____	st _____	s _____
st _____	f _____	att _____	s _____ ly
str _____	d _____	j _____ et	c _____
b _____ et	g _____	l _____	fig _____

Now write each word from memory.

_____   _____   _____   _____

_____   _____   _____   _____

_____   _____   _____   _____

_____   _____   _____   _____

_____   _____   _____   _____

Form the plurals of the following words.

truck _____   bull _____

jacket _____   figure _____

Now use some of the words from the boxes to complete the sentences.

1. We used a _____ to carry water from the river.

2. Can our small _____ pull such a large caravan?

3. Someone threw a stone at that window and put a _____ in it.

4. I'm not _____ whether Sally knows that girl.

43 Find the word in each line with a different letter pattern and write it in the box.

1. fries   own   owner   unknown   thrown   . . . .

2. eat   room   eating   heat   wheat   . . . .

3. others   mothers   instead   brothers   bothers   . . . .

4. out   about   shout   eat   trout   . . . .

5. end   tender   sending   pretend   scarce   . . . .

6. wore   store   core   more   thrown   . . . .

7. instead   bread   dread   others   steady   . . . .

8. room   roof   out   root   rooster   . . . .

9. scar   sending   scarf   scarce   scared   . . . .

10. more   fries   tries   cries   dries   . . . .

Match some of the words above with the meanings given below.

warmth . . . .   to save things to use later . . . .

frightened . . . .   covering of a building . . . .

to have something . . . .   to speak in a loud voice . . . .

annoys somebody . . . .   weeps . . . .

firm, not moving . . . .   to act as somebody else . . . .

44   Look carefully at the letter pattern in each box and use it to begin the following words.

purp — le ....

purp — ose ....

pol — ite ....

pol — ice ....

towe — l ....

towe — r ....

coco — a ....

coco — nut ....

wid — ow ....

wid — th ....

45   Practise writing the word **amp**.

_____   _____

Now use it to complete the following words.

c _____   ....

c _____ ing   ....

st _____   ....

st _____ ing   ....

tr _____   ....

tr _____ ing   ....

46 Use the word at the top of each box to make new words.

one

st _____
l _____ ly
z _____
sh_____
m _____ y
h _____ y

are

sh_____
sp_____
prep _____
d _____
r _____
_____ a

ear

f _____
y_____ s
n _____ ly
sp_____
w _____ ing
_____ ly

pea

_____ s
_____ k
_____ch
_____ r
_____ce

Now write each word from memory.

_____ _____ _____ _____

_____ _____ _____ _____

_____ _____ _____ _____

_____ _____ _____ _____

_____ _____ _____ _____

_____ _____ _____ _____

Find the words from the boxes that mean the opposite to the words below.

common . . . .

late . . . .

war . . . .

keep . . . .

Find the words from the boxes that fit correctly into the following spaces.

47 Look carefully at each letter pattern.

Now use this letter pattern to complete the words.

oze
d   n _____ _____
fr _____ _____

imb
l _____ _____
t   er _____ _____

ulle
p   d _____ _____
b   t _____ _____

oke
j _____ _____
br   n _____ _____

aw
cr   l _____ _____
h   k _____ _____

ank
th   ed _____ _____
     le _____ _____

ir
st _____ _____
sk   t _____ _____

cor
re   d _____ _____
s   e _____ _____

ax
t _____ _____
     e _____ _____

ail
h _____ _____
d   y _____ _____

ean
b _____ _____
m   t _____ _____

ight
midn _____ _____
m   y _____ _____

48 Practise writing the **kn** letter pattern.

Now use it to begin the following words.

_____ _____

kn
- ob . . . .
- ot . . . .
- ow . . . .
- it . . . .
- ee . . . .
- ight . . . .

49 Look carefully at the word in brackets at the end of each sentence.

Use this word to help you spell the word missing from each sentence.

_____ every day is one way of keeping fit. **(skip)**

We sometimes go _____ on a Friday evening. **(shop)**

Does it take much _____ to go by bus than by train? **(long)**

Please come and listen to our school choir _____ at the concert!

(sing)

The coach was _____ the team they must improve their game.

(tells)

50 Sometimes two words are put together to make a new word.
This new word is called a compound word.

Join these pieces together to make compound words.

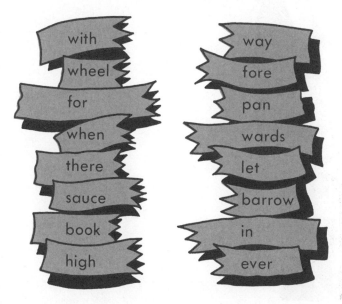

with   way

wheel   fore

for   pan

when   wards

there   let

sauce   barrow

book   in

high   ever

. . . .

. . . .

. . . .

. . . .

. . . .

. . . .

. . . .

. . . .

51 Practise writing the **ave** letter pattern.

Now use it to complete the following words.

sl _____

gr _____

tr _____ ller

....

....

....

52 Look carefully at the following words. Find the two words which go together and write them in the boxes.

dish

living

miss

dishes

ten

helping

kill

tenth

lived

missing

helped

killed

....

....

....

....

....

....

....

....

53 Practise writing the word **she**.

Now use it to begin the new words.

she ─── d

lf

lter

lves

pherd

....

....

....

....

54 The words in a dictionary are listed in alphabetical order. To put words in alphabetical order, use the first letter of each word. If the first letters are the same, use the second letter to put words in alphabetical order. If the second letters are the same use the third letter. If the first three letters are the same use the fourth letter.

Write each list of words in alphabetical order.

coach _____   eight _____

core _____   monkey _____

cough _____   enemy _____

coat _____   money _____

coast _____   month _____

cord _____   end _____

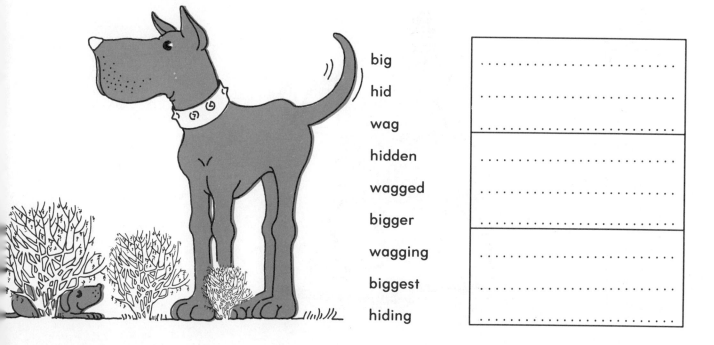

55 Look carefully at the following words. Find the word families and write them in the boxes.

big

hid

wag

hidden

wagged

bigger

wagging

biggest

hiding

56 Look carefully at the word in brackets at the end of each sentence.

Use this word to help you spell the word missing from each sentence.

Every birthday I have an increase in my _____ pocket-money. **(week)**

All day the tired explorers _____ for the lost city. **(hunting)**

Every morning the children enjoyed _____ to school. **(walked)**

The prizes were always _____ out during assembly. **(giving)**

When the supporters _____ with excitement, I knew their team had won. **(jumping)**

The _____ of the three brown bears was not at all friendly. **(larger)**

57 Practise writing the **ing** letter pattern.

Now make some new words beginning with the words in the boxes.

_____   _____

| shoot |
| sleep |
| will |
| meet |
| fix |
| slid |
| hid |
| rid |

ing

. . . .

. . . .

. . . .

. . . .

. . . .

. . . .

. . . .

. . . .

58 Find the word in each line with a different letter pattern and write it in the box.

1.	ford	toe	hoe	shoe	canoe	....
2.	leave	neck	weave	heave	heaven	....
3.	pitch	stitch	taste	hitch	kitchen	....
4.	oven	over	shovel	leave	overalls	....
5.	swam	swamp	swan	sway	mumps	....
6.	toast	coast	roast	boast	canoe	....
7.	taste	paste	waste	pitch	haste	....
8.	neck	deck	oven	speck	wreck	....
9.	jumps	swan	lumps	mumps	stumps	....
10.	boast	ford	afford	border	order	....

Match some of the words above with the meanings given below.

used for digging	....	to spoil	....
marshy ground	....	a small boat	....
warmed, crisp bread	....	the edge	....
pieces of something, swellings	....	a room where food is cooked	....
to make cloth from threads	....	used to stick things together	....

59 Look carefully at the following words.

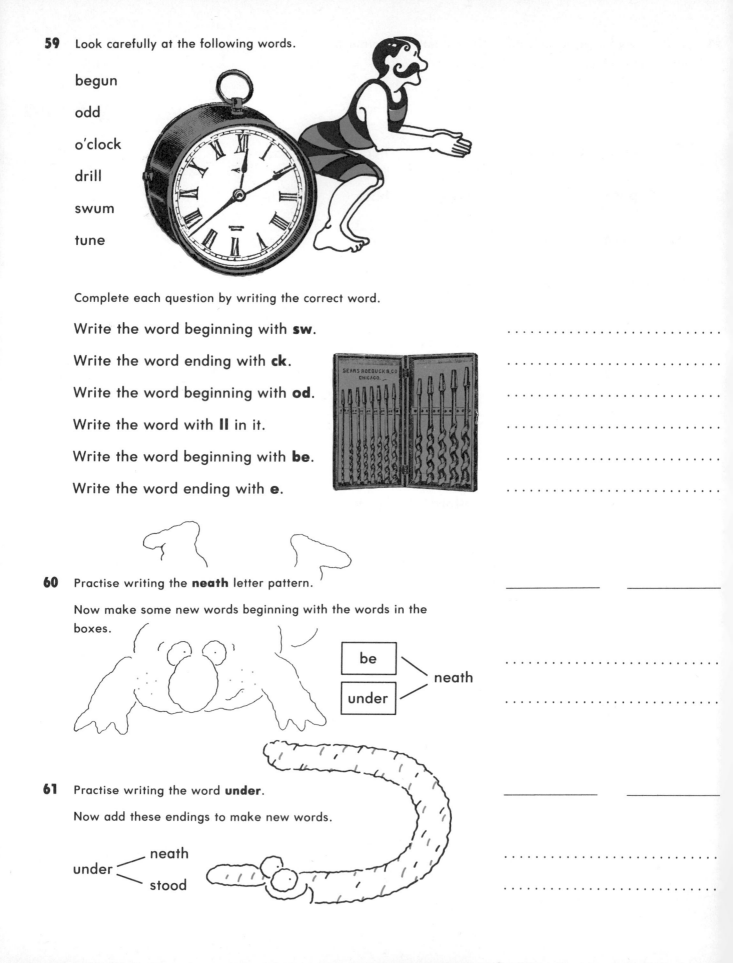

begun

odd

o'clock

drill

swum

tune

Complete each question by writing the correct word.

Write the word beginning with **sw**.

. . . .

Write the word ending with **ck**.

. . . .

Write the word beginning with **od**.

. . . .

Write the word with **ll** in it.

. . . .

Write the word beginning with **be**.

. . . .

Write the word ending with **e**.

. . . .

60 Practise writing the **neath** letter pattern.

_____   _____

Now make some new words beginning with the words in the boxes.

be ⟩ neath
under ⟩

. . . .

. . . .

61 Practise writing the word **under**.

_____   _____

Now add these endings to make new words.

under ⟨ neath
        stood

. . . .

. . . .

62 Read the advertisement David wanted to place in the lost and found column of his school newspaper. He made seven spelling mistakes.

Draw a line under each spelling mistake.

LOST

I lost my blue jacket at school last Wedenesday. That's unusual for me becouse I never lose anything. My jacket is unlike any you have every seen. I painted the name of my favourite group, 'The Stargazers', on the back in pink and perple. The jacket would be hard to replace. I'd be unabel to make another one exactly like it. If you find the jacket, please retern it to me. Untill then, you'll see a very unhappy face around the school.

Now write the seven misspelled words correctly.

_____   _____   _____   _____

_____   _____   _____

Complete the following story by filling in the gaps with words
which make sense.

You may need to use your dictionary to help you spell a word.
Remember to write each word from memory.

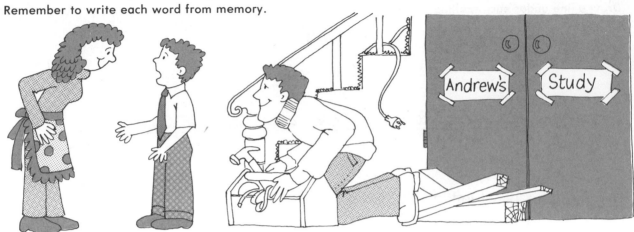

A ROOM FOR ANDREW

It was very difficult for Andrew. He _____ a boy who liked things to be

_____ in order. Unfortunately, he had two younger _____ who

could never be trusted to leave _____ things alone. All the time he was

_____ school he worried about what might have _____ while he

was away. One day his _____ had been stuck into his album with

_____. They were even on the wrong pages. _____ mother

knew that he was worried. "I _____ what we will do. We will turn

_____ cupboard under the stairs into a study _____ Andrew".

There was just room for a _____ desk and chair but the wall was

_____ with shelves.

The day after the trouble _____ the stamps, Andrew's Dad came home

from _____ and got the room ready for Andrew's _____ . That

afternoon when Andrew had run home _____ school, he quickly realised that

all his _____ had disappeared. "What have you done with

_____ my things?" he screamed. But then he _____ the notice

Mum had put on the _____ to the cupboard under the stairs. "Oh!"

_____ said. He was too surprised and too _____ to say any

more. But his Mum _____ Dad knew that they had done the

_____ thing.

64 The words in a dictionary are listed in alphabetical order. To put words in alphabetical order, use the first letter of each word. If the first letters are the same, use the second letter to put words in alphabetical order. If the second letters are the same use the third letter. If the first three letters are the same use the fourth letter.

Write each list of words in alphabetical order.

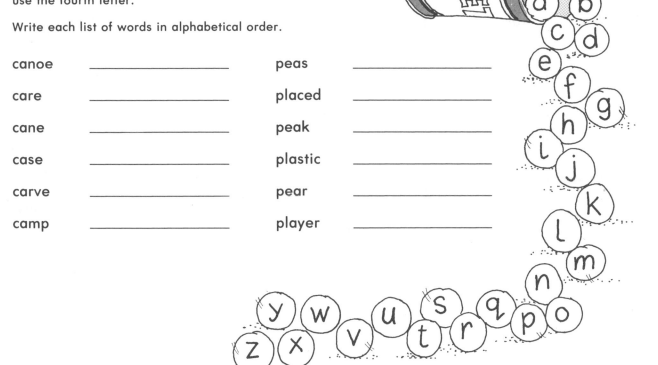

canoe   _____

care   _____

cane   _____

case   _____

carve   _____

camp   _____

peas   _____

placed   _____

peak   _____

plastic _____

pear   _____

player   _____

65 Look carefully at the following words. Find the word families and write them in the boxes.

stop

easy

luck

stopped

easier

lucky

stopping

easiest

luckily

66 Look carefully at the word next to each box.

Now use this word to complete the words in the box.

tal _____	
wal _____	king

_____ st	
choco _____	late

pil _____	
s _____ ly	low

gol _____	
har _____	den

_____ ing	
_____ ile	miss

. . . .

. . . .

. . . .

. . . .

. . . .

. . . .

. . . .

. . . .

. . . .

. . . .

67 Look carefully at the following words. Find the word families
and write them in the boxes.

swim

stay

hurried

stayed

swimmer

hurries

swimming

staying

hurrying

. . . .

. . . .

. . . .

. . . .

. . . .

. . . .

. . . .

. . . .

68 Look carefully at the word in brackets at the end of each sentence.

Use this word to help you spell the word missing from each sentence.

My grandmother was much _____ than my mother. **(oldest)**

The mountain _____ was killed in a sudden rock fall. **(climbed)**

To save me, the brave dog swam the _____ of the river. **(wide)**

Luckily for Jason he _____ his driving test last Tuesday.

(passing)

The school bus _____ up most of the children at the first corner.

(picking)

69 Practise writing the **ain** letter pattern.   _____   _____

Now write the words beginning with the letters in the balloons.

· ·

· ·

· ·

· ·

· ·

70 Practise writing the **ide** letter pattern.   _____   _____

Now make some new words beginning with the letters in the boxes.

· ·

· ·

· ·

· ·

· ·

71 Practise writing the **ame** letter pattern.

Now write the words beginning with the letters in the balloons.

n   t   fr   l   fl

ame

_____   _____

. . . .

. . . .

. . . .

. . . .

72 Practise writing the word **ink**.

Now make some new words beginning with the letters in the boxes.

s

p

th

shr

ink

_____   _____

. . . .

. . . .

. . . .

. . . .

73 Look carefully at the word in brackets at the end of each sentence.

Use this word to help you spell the word missing from the sentence.

I suppose the baby was _____ William after his father. **(name**

We heard a loud _____ coming from behind the trees. **(crying**

All the people were _____ at the antics of the monkey. **(smile**

I'm sorry I _____ the cup and saucer on the floor. **(drop)**

Every Friday the teacher took the children _____ at the rink.

(skate)

74 Complete the following story by filling in the gaps with words which make sense.

You may need to use your dictionary to help you spell a word.

Remember to write each word from memory.

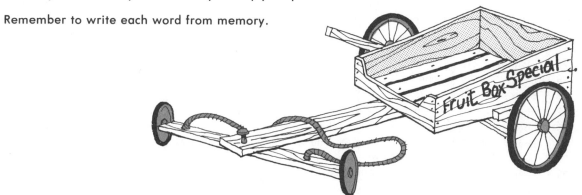

A SURPRISE FOR SARAH

All summer Sarah had sat at the _____ watching her friends out there on

their _____ and their roller-skates speeding faster and _____ from

the top of the hill in _____ park. She had been kept indoors for _____

since her accident when she had been _____ down by a car as she ran

_____ the pink ice-cream van. It was her _____ next day and she

would have liked _____ bike but she knew there was no _____.

When she woke up next morning, there, _____ her bed was the last thing she

_____ to see—a long wooden billy-cart with _____ ropes for

steering and a real hand _____. Dad looked round the door as Sarah

_____ with pleasure. "You can go faster on _____," said Dad.

Sarah offered rides to her _____. She even lent the billy-cart to younger

_____.

All the boys and girls who borrowed the billy-cart _____ it up before they

reached the bottom _____ the hill, but Sarah never once overturned,

_____ when it was loaded with four or _____ younger children

who jumped and shouted as _____ drove. For them it was just very

_____, but for Sarah it was more, it _____ the freedom that she

thought she had _____ for ever.

INDEX

These are all the words in this book. The numbers tell you in which games the words appear. You may need this list when looking for a special word.